How People Use Electricity

How Electric Energy Works

**DEVELOPED IN COOPERATION
WITH**

LOUISVILLE SCIENCE CENTER
LOUISVILLE, KENTUCKY

Copyright © 1995 by Scholastic Inc.   All rights reserved. Published by Scholastic Inc.   Printed in the U.S.A.
ISBN 0-590-27698-0
2 3 4 5 6 7 8 9 10   09   01 00 99 98 97 96 95

PEOPLE APPLY TOOLS, SKILLS, AND SCIENTIFIC KNOWLEDGE TO SOLVE PROBLEMS AND EXTEND HUMAN CAPABILITIES.

How People Use Electricity

People have invented systems that generate, transmit, and use electricity.

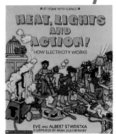

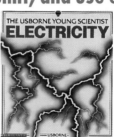

Electricity occurs as static electricity or as current electricity running through a circuit.

People use the properties of magnetism to generate electricity.

Electricity can be changed into other forms of energy.

Think Tank: Designing an Electric Toy Exploration Lab

What if . . .

. . . you woke up one morning and none of the electric devices in your home worked? No alarm clock waking up your family, no lights, possibly no stove or hot water. What if the whole day was like that? Everywhere you went and everything you did had to be done without electricity.

Your life would change in many more ways than you can imagine.

What do you know about electricity?

You probably use electricity many times every day. In fact, you're probably using it right this minute. Work with your class to make a list of what you already know about electricity.

What do you want to know?

Make a second list with your class. This time, list questions you have about electricity. For example, why is that person's hair standing on end?

How will you find out?

You'll work in teams as you do hands-on explorations that will help you discover answers to many of your questions. You'll share what you learn with other teams in your class. You'll also find out what other scientists have discovered about electricity.

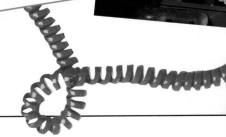

Using scientific methods:

The table of contents on pages 2 and 3 shows the problems you're going to solve in this unit. Each problem you solve will help you solve the ones that come after it. In each exploration lesson, you and your team will use scientific methods to solve the problem:

• You'll make a *hypothesis* — a prediction — about possible answers to the problem.

• You'll do a *hands-on exploration* — maybe two — that will help you test your hypothesis. You'll learn how to generate electric energy and how to change it to other forms of energy.

• You'll *record data* you collect.

• You'll *draw conclusions* from your data.

• You'll *compare* your conclusions to those of other teams in your class.

• You'll *apply* your conclusions to your own life.

How Do You Use Electricity?

The alarm goes off, and you jump out of bed and switch on the light. You turn on the radio for the weather report to see what you'll need to wear. You want the jeans that are still in the clothes dryer. You fix yourself some toast and get some orange juice from the refrigerator. You've been awake five minutes. How many times have you used electricity?

Exploration:

Find out how you depend on electricity.

❶ Think of what you did yesterday evening. Make a list of anything you did that involved using electricity.

❷ Divide the activities on your list into those that used electricity from outlets in the wall and those that used batteries.

❸ Now go through your list. Could you have done any of the things *without* using electricity? How?

Interpret your results.

• What is the main difference between appliances that plug into the wall and those that use batteries?

• Which of the ways you could do things *without* electricity might have been used a hundred years ago? Do those ways have any advantages? any disadvantages?

• What do you think would be the greatest change in your life if you lived without electricity?

▲ In July 1977 New York City went without electricity for over 12 hours. What do you think were some effects of the blackout?

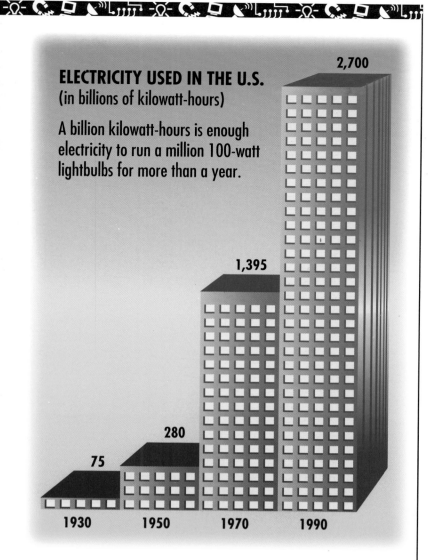

ELECTRICITY USED IN THE U.S.
(in billions of kilowatt-hours)

A billion kilowatt-hours is enough electricity to run a million 100-watt lightbulbs for more than a year.

2,700

1,395

280

75

1930   1950   1970   1990

Exploration Connection:
Interpreting graphs

Whether you live in a big city or in the country, you probably have electricity in your home. You can flick a switch and a lamp will light up. But it hasn't always been like this. The first electric company was set up in New York City in 1882. This company sent electricity to several buildings. It supplied power for 800 light bulbs.

The more people found out about electricity, the more they used it. Look at the graph. It shows how much electricity was used in the United States during four different years. What reasons can you think of to explain why more electricity is used now than in 1930? than in 1970?

▶ One of the first uses of electricity to light an outdoor area

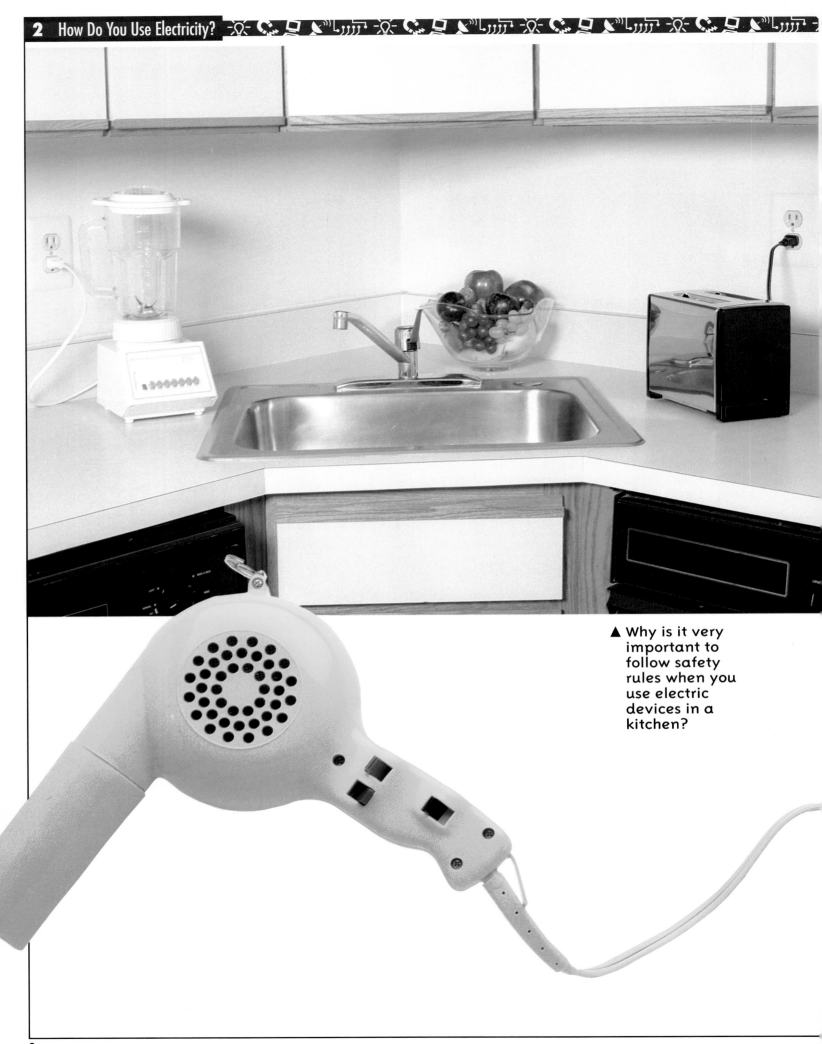

▲ Why is it very important to follow safety rules when you use electric devices in a kitchen?

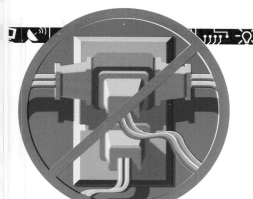

Why shouldn't you do the things shown in the diagrams?

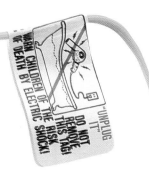

▼ Many electric devices are labeled with warnings against unsafe use.

Closer to Home: Using electricity safely

Electricity is one of the most useful forms of energy. But it can be very dangerous if it isn't used properly—it can cause fires and electric shocks. There are some important things you should remember if you handle electric switches or sockets. They're important because they could save your life.

Water and electricity don't mix. If your hands are wet or if you're standing on a wet floor, don't touch an electric switch or use an electric device. Electricity can travel through water. If you want to use a radio in the bathroom, use a battery-powered one—it doesn't use enough electricity to harm you.

Keep electricity where it belongs—in wires or in devices. If the cords are frayed or cracked, they're dangerous. If you ever have to clean or repair an electric device, make sure it's unplugged first.

In the United States, a group called Underwriters Laboratories, or UL, sets safety rules for devices that use electricity. When a device passes the safety rules, it's marked saying that it's approved by UL. If you're going to buy an electric device, make sure it's UL-approved.

Think before you plug a lot of things into one outlet. Is there another outlet you could use? Plugging too many devices into one socket can blow a fuse or even start a fire.

- If you use a hair dryer in the bathroom, what safety tips should you follow?

- What do you think are some things UL checks before they approve a device?

Think!

If you could use only three electric devices in your home, what would they be? Explain your choices.

What Is Electricity?

What is electricity? Where does it come from? One of the easiest ways to find out about electricity is to watch it when it isn't traveling to a device. That kind of electricity is called <u>static electricity</u>. If you've ever slid across a carpet and felt a shock when you touched a door handle, you've felt static electricity.

Exploration:
Make static electricity.

You need:

2 balloons
Thread
Wool
Goggles

❶ Blow up each balloon, and tie it with thread so that it remains inflated.

❷ Rub one balloon several times against the wool. Now place it on the wall and let go. Observe and record what happens. ✏

❸ Now rub both balloons against the wool several times. Hold the thread from a balloon in each hand so that the sides you rubbed on the wool are next to each other. Bring the balloons together. Observe what happens. ✏

Interpret your results.

• What happened to the balloon when you put it on the wall? How long did the effect last? If you were to rub the balloon for a longer time, do you think the effect would last longer? **Try it!**

• What happened when you put the two balloons near each other? Do you think you could make the effect stronger if you rubbed the balloons for a longer time? **Try it!**

• When you rub a balloon, you make static electricity on its surface. Based on your results, what are two effects of static electricity?

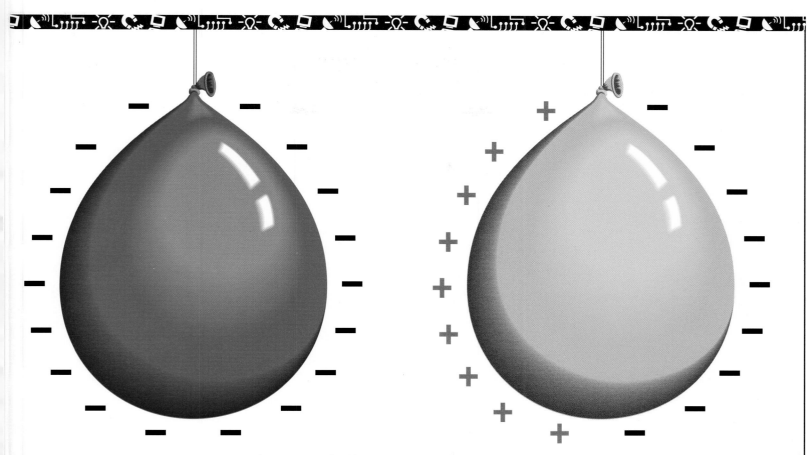

▲ The green balloon was rubbed and the orange balloon wasn't. The green balloon's single charge attracts the opposite charge from the orange balloon. What happens?

Exploration Connection: Using reference books

When you made static electricity by rubbing the balloon against the wool, the balloon and the wool each had a different electric <u>charge</u>. Electricity has two different charges: positive and negative. Charges that are the same push each other away. Charges that are different pull each other closer. When you rubbed the balloon and put it on the wall, did the wall and the balloon have the same charge or a different charge? What will happen if you rub your hands over a balloon that has static electricity? **Try it!** You can find out why by reading pages 8–11 of *Heat, Lights and Action!*

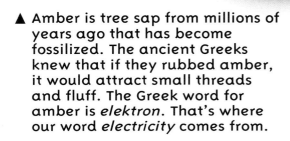

▲ Amber is tree sap from millions of years ago that has become fossilized. The ancient Greeks knew that if they rubbed amber, it would attract small threads and fluff. The Greek word for amber is *elektron*. That's where our word *electricity* comes from.

Closer to Home:
Lightning

The static electricity on a balloon won't hurt you. The electric shock that you can get from a doorknob is simply annoying. But static electricity isn't always harmless. It can heat up the air so that it's much hotter than the surface of the sun. It can even melt iron—and it does it in a flash.

In a thunderstorm, static electricity gathers at the bottom of a thundercloud. It's attracted to the earth, just as the balloon in the Exploration was attracted to the wall. The electricity jumps to the ground as a spark of lightning.

The sound of thunder is made when the air around the lightning is heated up. The closer you are to the lightning, the louder the thunder is. There's a good way to tell how far away lightning is. Light travels much, much faster than sound, so you can see lightning before you hear it. For every second you can count between seeing the lightning and hearing it, the lightning is one fifth of a mile away from you. If it takes five seconds before you hear thunder, how far away is the lightning?

Around the world, lightning strikes the earth about one hundred times each second. In the United States, lightning causes about one hundred deaths each year. So it's a good idea to know some simple safety rules you can follow if you're caught in a thunderstorm.

Most tall buildings have lightning rods. Because the lightning rod is closest to the thundercloud, it will attract any lightning that would be likely to hit the building. The electricity flows through the rod and into the ground.

1. Lightning is attracted to the tallest object in an area. If you're in the open, crouch down. Stay away from tall trees.

2. If you're riding a bike, get off the bike and move away from it (and any other metal objects).

3. If you're swimming, get out of the water as soon as you hear thunder.

• You shouldn't use the telephone during a thunderstorm, except in an emergency. Why wouldn't it be safe?

• A boat isn't very tall. Why is it dangerous to be on a boat in the middle of a lake when there's a thunderstorm?

Think!

Sometimes your clothes stick to each other even though they're dry. Why?

How Can Electricity Move?

When you play a radio for a long time, the batteries run down—so you put new batteries in. Radios don't use much electricity. Heaters, stoves, and lights use much more. You probably use some of these devices a lot. In fact, you're good at using up electricity. How about making your own for a change?

Exploration:
Make a battery.

You need:

6 plastic cups
6 short copper wires
6 short aluminum wires
4 alligator clips
2 long wires
LED   Teaspoon
Salt   Hot water

❶ Line up the six cups in a row.

❷ Make five pairs of wires: each is a short copper wire and a short aluminum wire twisted together at one end. Spread the other ends apart. Hang the pairs where the cups touch, making sure there's a copper wire and an aluminum wire in each cup (except the two end cups).

❸ Bend the other short wires into hooks, and hang them in the end cups so that each cup has copper and aluminum in it.

❹ Fasten an alligator clip to each end of each long wire. Attach one clip to the copper hook. Attach the other end of that wire to the longer leg of the LED. Attach a clip on the other wire to the aluminum hook. Attach the other end of the wire to the shorter leg of the LED.

❺ Fill each cup 3/4 full with hot water. Add 4 spoonfuls of salt to each cup. Cup your hands around the LED and look at it. Record your observations. ✏️

Interpret your results.

- In what ways is your battery like a flashlight battery? In what ways is it different?

- What do you think would happen if you connected only one leg of the LED to the battery? **Try it!**

- What materials did electricity move through?

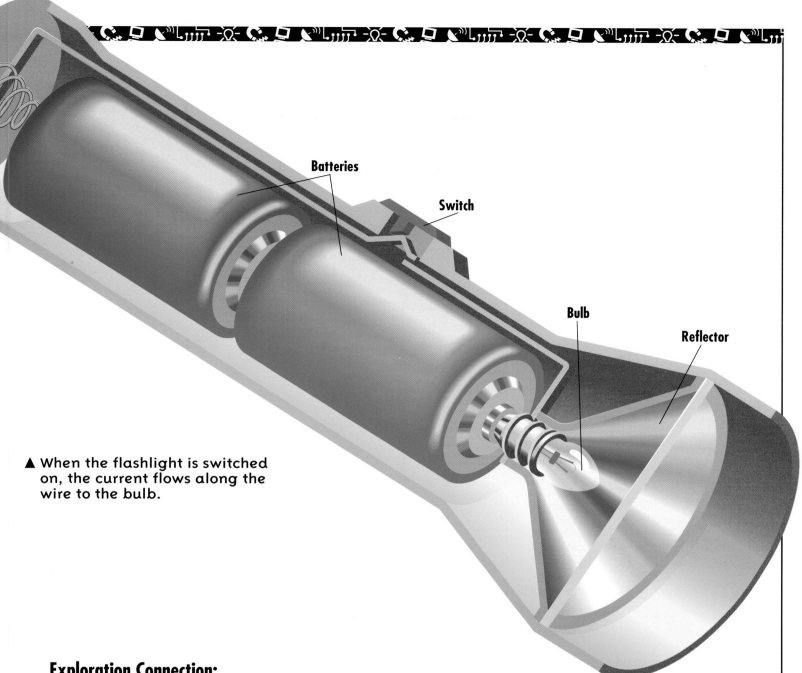

Batteries

Switch

Bulb

Reflector

▲ When the flashlight is switched on, the current flows along the wire to the bulb.

Exploration Connection:
Interpreting diagrams

When you connect a battery to a light bulb or an LED, you make a <u>circuit</u>. Every part of the circuit must be joined to the next part, or electricity can't pass through it. If you removed the wires that joined two cups in your saltwater battery, do you think the LED would light up? **Try it!**

Look at the diagram of the flashlight. It shows the circuit when it isn't complete. How does the switch control the electricity traveling through the circuit?

For some devices, such as flashlight bulbs, it doesn't matter which way the electricity travels. But some things that run on electricity won't work unless the electricity going through them is traveling in the right direction. That's why a radio has a diagram in the battery compartment showing which way the batteries should face. LEDs are other things that must be connected the right way in a circuit. If you connected the LED in the Exploration the other way around, what do you think would happen?

You made your saltwater battery with six parts. Each part was a cup of salt water with metal wires. And each part was a battery itself. So you really made six batteries connected together. You've probably noticed that different devices—radios and flashlights, for example— use different numbers of batteries. Why?

Exploration:
Find out how powerful your battery is.

You need:

Saltwater battery
LED
Teaspoon

❶ Stir all of the salt water in the battery cells you made in the first Exploration. Now take one of the cups and put the copper and the aluminum hooks in it. Attach one long wire between the copper hook and the longer leg of the LED.

❷ Attach one end of the other long wire to the aluminum hook, and the other end of that wire to the shorter leg of the LED. You now have a single saltwater battery. Cup your hands around the LED. Does the LED light up? ✏

❸ Add on another cup of salt water and one of the copper-aluminum pairs of wires to make a two-part battery. Record what happens to the LED. ✏

❹ Repeat step 3, adding cups to make a three-part, four-part, five-part, and six-part battery. ✏

Interpret your results.

• What happened to the LED when you added more parts to your battery?

• What happens when you connect batteries together?

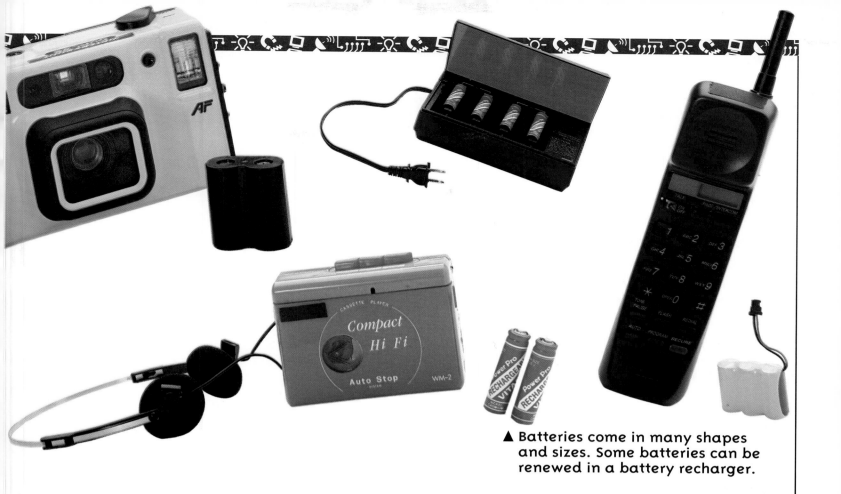

▲ Batteries come in many shapes and sizes. Some batteries can be renewed in a battery recharger.

Closer to Home:
Electricity in your pocket!

Batteries are packages of chemicals that make it easy to carry electricity any place you go. Small batteries run portable radios, televisions, and computers. What other things do you use that run on batteries?

Many forms of transportation use electricity. Although car engines use gasoline as fuel, they need electricity, too. That's why cars have batteries. Airplanes and ships also use batteries for their engines and for lights. Even space shuttles use batteries.

Batteries can improve people's lives in other ways, too. Some people who have heart problems use tiny battery-powered devices to keep their hearts beating. Batteries also help people who use hearing aids.

Americans use—and throw away—about two billion batteries each year. Because they contain dangerous chemicals, these batteries can harm the environment. One solution to this problem is to use batteries that can be recharged. After these batteries have run down, they can be plugged into a wall outlet, and they become good as new.

• How would your life change if you had to plug all your battery-operated devices into wall outlets? Explain your answer.

• Is the battery in a car a kind of rechargeable battery? How do you know?

Why don't you run all the electric devices in your home with batteries?

What Can Electricity Travel Through?

When electricity flows through a circuit, it's called an electric <u>current</u>. It's something like water flowing through a pipe to a faucet. The water won't travel to the faucet if it doesn't have the pipe to travel through. Electricity also needs something that it can travel through. In Lesson 4, electricity traveled through aluminum and copper. What else do you think electricity can travel through?

Negative (−)

Positive (+)

(+)

(−)

Exploration:
Make a test unit.

You need:
2 "D" batteries
2 battery holders
1 short copper wire
Red wire with alligator clip
Black wire with alligator clip
LED

❶ Place a battery in each holder. Connect the two battery holders using the short copper wire. Make sure that each battery faces in the same direction as in the photograph.

❷ Connect the free end of the red wire to the positive terminal of the battery holder. Connect the free end of the black wire to the negative terminal.

❸ Clip the red wire to the longer leg of the LED.

❹ Predict what will happen if you touch the clip on the black wire to the shorter leg of the LED. Test your prediction. ✎

Interpret your results.

• Electricity travels in one direction through a circuit. What do you think would happen to your circuit if you attached the battery holders so that the same terminals of each battery were connected? **Try it!**

• Why is it helpful to have different-colored wires in the test unit?

• How could you use this circuit to find out if electricity will travel through a material?

Exploration Connection:
Using reference books

The wires you used in the Exploration are made of copper. So are the wires that run through your home and the wires that connect electric devices to outlets. The only metal that carries electricity better than copper is silver. Why do you think silver isn't usually used for wires?

Copper wires can carry a lot of electric current. But if they carry too much, they'll get too hot. They could even start a fire. That's why homes have <u>fuses</u> for their circuits. If too many devices are turned on, a fuse will melt and stop the flow of electricity. You can find out how fuses work by reading page 36 in *Heat, Lights and Action*!

▲ Wall outlets are connected to wires that carry electricity through your home; the prongs of a plug are connected to wires that carry electricity to an electric device.

What materials are used to keep the electric current in your house from harming you? Look at some plugs, outlets, and wires that carry electricity. What different materials are they made of? Your test unit can let you find out which materials will carry electricity.

Exploration:
Find out what will carry electricity.

You need:

Test unit
Coins
Pencil
Small items of
    your own

❶ Check that the LED lights up when a clip is attached to each leg.

❷ Take the clip off one leg of the LED. Clip it onto a coin. Now touch a different part of the coin to the leg of the LED. Record what happens. ✎

❸ Repeat step 2 using other coins, and then the pencil. Try the wood part, the eraser, and the pencil point. Record your observations. ✎

❹ Repeat step 2 using as many small items as you can think of (and have handy). ✎

Interpret your results.

• What can you tell about a material that allowed the LED to light up?

• How were the materials that allowed the LED to light up alike?

• What prediction can you make about which materials will carry electricity?

• Did any of the results surprise you? If so, why?

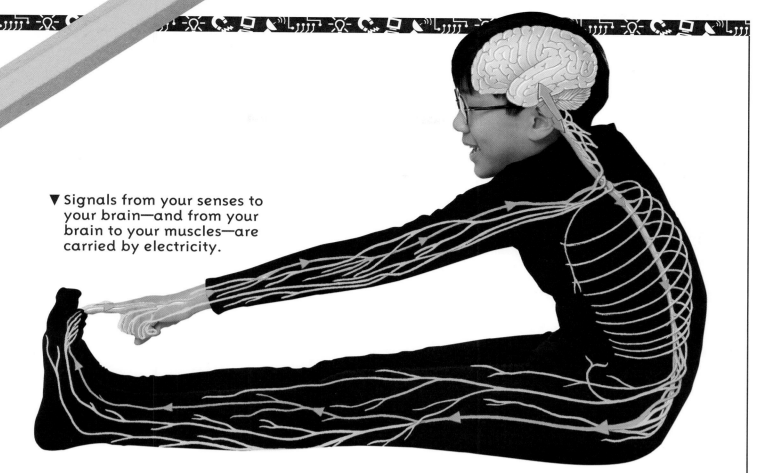

▼ Signals from your senses to your brain—and from your brain to your muscles—are carried by electricity.

Closer to Home: You're a conductor.

A material that lets electricity travel through it is called a <u>conductor</u>. You're a conductor. That's why electricity can be dangerous to you. If you weren't a conductor, you wouldn't be able to get electric shocks. But you can get electric shocks. They happen if a lot of electricity travels through your body. If there's enough electricity, a shock can seriously harm you—or even kill you.

Everything you do depends on electricity traveling through your body. Whenever you see, hear, smell, taste, or feel anything, a message travels to your brain. Whenever you move, a message travels *from* your brain. Every message travels along nerves. Your nerves don't look like telephone wires, but they act a little bit like them. Each message to or from your brain travels as electricity!

Look at the diagram. When you touch something with your finger, an electric signal is sent from your finger to your brain. If you decide to move your toe, your brain sends an electric signal to the muscles that control it.

• You're a conductor, but how well do you conduct electricity? If you had tested your finger in the Exploration, what do you think would have happened? **Try it!**

• When your brain sends and receives messages, do the messages use a large or a small amount of electricity? Why do you think so?

Think!

Most electric cords are made of copper wrapped in plastic. What other kinds of cords might work?

What Paths Can Electricity Take?

Electric current will only flow through certain materials. It will only flow if it has somewhere to go. When a current travels through a wire, the wire is part of a circuit. If the circuit is broken, what happens? Are all circuits the same?

Exploration:
Make series and parallel circuits.

You need:

Test unit
2 lamp holders
2 flashlight bulbs
2 copper wires

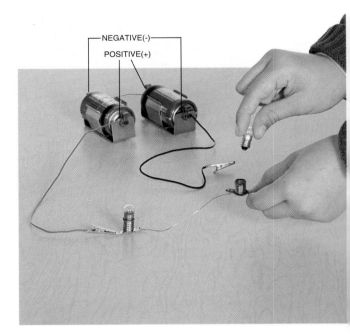

NEGATIVE(-)
POSITIVE(+)

❶ Disconnect the LED from the wires of the test unit you made in Lesson 5. The batteries, wires, and clips are your battery pack.

❷ Use the clip to attach the red wire to one end of a lamp holder. Attach the black wire to one end of the other lamp holder.

❸ Use one copper wire to connect the unused ends of the two lamp holders. Screw the bulbs into the lamp holders. You've made a <u>series</u> circuit. Record what happens.

❹ Disconnect the lamp holders from the series circuit. Use one of the copper wires to connect one end of each lamp holder. Connect the other two ends with the other copper wire.

❺ Now attach the wires from the battery pack to the ends of one of the lamp holders. You've made a <u>parallel</u> circuit. Record what happens.

Interpret your results.

- What did the electric current pass through to reach each bulb in each of the circuits? If you removed one bulb from each circuit, what would happen to the circuit? What would happen to the other bulb? **Try it!**

- When you blow a fuse in the kitchen, you may still be able to use electricity in the living room. What does that tell you about the circuit in your home?

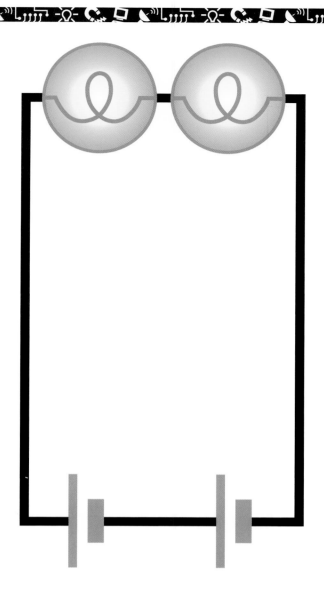

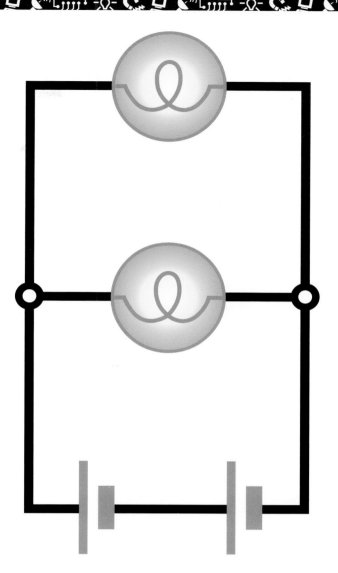

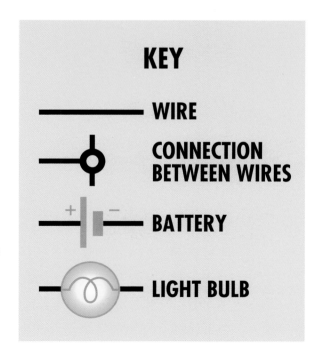

▲ Trace the path of the electric current through each circuit with your finger.

Exploration Connection:
Interpreting diagrams

Electrical engineers who design circuits for video games, telephones, and all kinds of electric devices use special symbols to make their work easier. Use the key to read the diagrams on this page. Which one shows the series circuit from the Exploration? Which one shows the parallel circuit?

KEY

────────── WIRE

──●── CONNECTION BETWEEN WIRES

──+|−── BATTERY

──◯── LIGHT BULB

When you made a series circuit, you connected two bulbs in a row. The current had to pass through one bulb to reach the other. In your parallel circuit, each bulb was connected by itself to the battery pack. Suppose you wanted to switch the bulbs on and off one at a time. Which kind of circuit would let you control each bulb separately?

Exploration:
Turn a circuit on and off.

You need:

4 paper fasteners

2 metal paper clips

2 small pieces of cardboard

4 short wires

Series circuit

Parallel circuit

❶ Attach a paper clip to a piece of cardboard with a paper fastener. Then push another paper fastener through the cardboard so that it just touches the paper clip.

❷ Attach a wire to each paper fastener on the cardboard. You've made a switch. Current will only flow through the switch if the paper clip touches both paper fasteners.

❸ Repeat steps 1 and 2 to make another switch.

❹ Try different ways of putting your switches in the series circuit you made. Can you turn the bulbs on and off? Can you turn them on and off separately?

❺ Repeat step 4 for the parallel circuit you made.

Interpret your results.

- How did you turn the bulbs on and off in the series circuit? How many switches did you need?

- Can you turn the bulbs in a series circuit on and off separately?

- How did you turn the bulbs on and off in the parallel circuit? How many switches did you need?

- Can you turn the bulbs in a parallel circuit on and off separately?

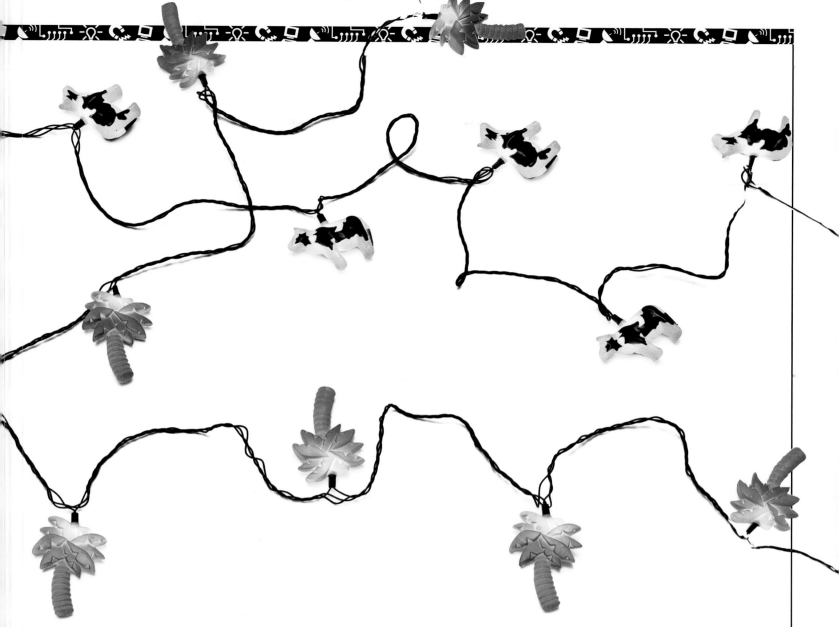

Closer to Home:
Your electric neighborhood

Perhaps you've turned on one appliance too many, and caused too much current to go through the wires. Luckily, a fuse blew, breaking the circuit. This prevented the wires from heating up and starting a fire.

What happened to the electricity next door when your fuse blew? What happened down the street? Nothing! The problem in your home didn't affect anybody else's supply of electricity.

The apartments in an apartment building are on a parallel circuit. So are the houses on a short street. That's why there can still be electricity next door when the electricity in your home fails.

• Sometimes all the lights in an apartment building go out. Even so, the nearby buildings aren't affected. Could the different buildings be on the same circuit? Explain.

• What problems might occur if several homes were part of a series circuit?

You want to set up a string of party lights. Would you use a series circuit or a parallel circuit? Why?

What Can Magnets Do?

There's one thing that's true of any circuit: It must be made of materials that are conductors. Electricity won't travel if it doesn't have a conductor to travel through. What kind of energy do you think might be able to travel without having something to travel through?

Exploration:
Discover the properties of magnets.

You need:

Magnet
Small items
Paper
Cup
Water

❶ Use the magnet with some small items. What do you observe?

❷ See if you get the same results as you did in step 1 when you place a sheet of paper between the magnet and the items.

❸ Pour water into the cup so that it is half full. See if the magnet and the items act the same way underwater as they did in step 1.

❹ Work with another group to see how magnets act with each other.

Interpret your results.

• Does a magnet have to touch an object to have an effect on it?

• Can a magnet's energy travel through air? water? What other materials might it travel through? **Try it!**

• What items did the magnet affect? What did those items have in common?

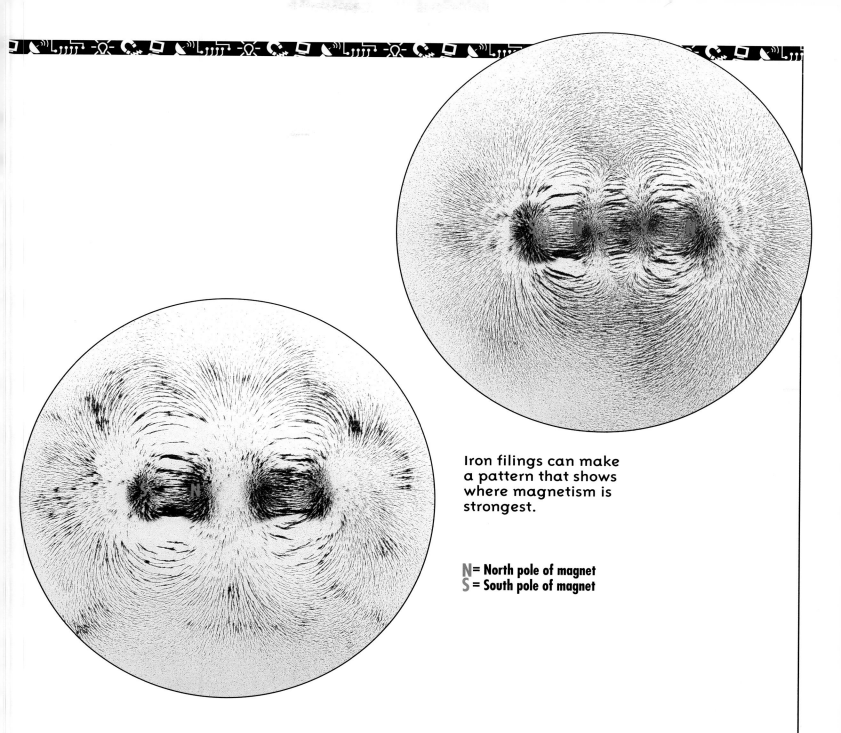

Iron filings can make a pattern that shows where magnetism is strongest.

N = North pole of magnet
S = South pole of magnet

Exploration Connection:
Interpreting diagrams

Every magnet has a north pole and a south pole. These poles are at the ends of the magnet. When the poles of two different magnets are near each other, they either pull each other closer or push each other away. If one of the poles is north and the other is south, they'll pull each other closer. If the poles are both the same, they'll push each other away. **Try it!**

Look at the top diagram. It shows iron filings—iron that's ground into a powder—sprinkled into a pan of oil. There are two magnets under the pan. The filings gather in places where the magnets are strongest. Which parts of a magnet are strongest? Now look at the lower diagram. Which pole of the unmarked magnet do you think is north and which is south? Explain your thinking.

Closer to Home:
Magnetism you can see

If you live in one of the northernmost states or in Canada, this Closer to Home is close to your home. You've probably been lucky enough to see the beautiful light show in the sky called the Northern Lights. The Northern Lights shine in the sky at heights of between 100 and 1,000 kilometers (60 and 600 miles). They happen when electrically charged particles from the sun hit particles in Earth's atmosphere. When the particles bump into each other, they give off light. The most common color of these lights is green, but they can also be red or purple.

The earth acts like a magnet, and like the magnet you used in the Exploration, its pull is strongest at its magnetic poles, near the North Pole and South Pole. The particles from the sun are pulled to the strongest part of the earth's magnetism. That's why the Northern Lights only exist in the far north.

- Look at the map. Where else in the world can the Northern Lights be seen?

- Do you think there are "Southern Lights," too? Explain your answer.

Think!

How could magnets be used to make an object "float" in the air?

▼The lighter area on the map shows the parts of the world from which you can sometimes see the Northern Lights.

How Is Electricity Used to Make Magnets?

When you made static electricity on balloons, you found that it pushes and pulls. When you used two magnets together, you discovered that they can push and pull, too. What might magnets and electricity have to do with each other?

Exploration:
Observe the effects of electricity in a coil.

You need:
Enameled copper wire
Sandpaper
Battery pack
Nail
Tape
Paper clips
Staples

❶ Rub about 2 cm of each end of the copper wire with sandpaper until they're shiny.

❷ Attach one wire from the battery pack to one end of the copper wire.

❸ Tape the copper wire to the nail, and then wind it about 60 times around the nail. Tape the coil you've made so that it doesn't unwind.

❹ Attach the free end of the copper wire to the free wire from the battery pack. Record what happens when you touch the nail to a paper clip.

❺ Repeat step 4 with different numbers of paper clips.

Interpret your results.

• Why was it important to rub the ends of the copper wire with sandpaper?

• What does a coil carrying electric current do?

• How could you make the coil stronger or weaker? Compare the number of staples you can pick up with the nail. **Try it!**

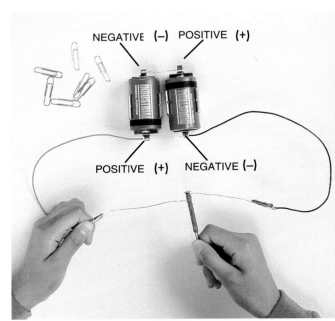

NEGATIVE (−) POSITIVE (+)

POSITIVE (+) NEGATIVE (−)

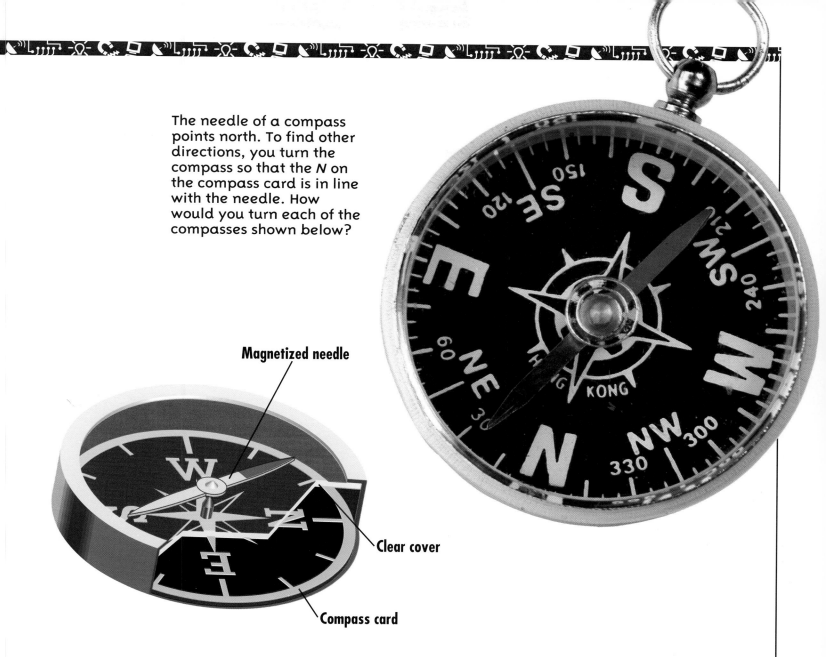

The needle of a compass points north. To find other directions, you turn the compass so that the *N* on the compass card is in line with the needle. How would you turn each of the compasses shown below?

Magnetized needle

Clear cover

Compass card

Exploration Connection:
Interpreting diagrams

Every magnet has a north pole and a south pole—and so does the planet you live on. Earth acts like a giant magnet. Opposite poles of magnets attract each other. So if a magnet can move freely, one pole will always point to Earth's magnetic North Pole, and the other will point to the magnetic South Pole. That's why a compass works—the compass needle is a magnet.

The kind of compass used by campers and hikers hasn't changed much since it was invented in China a thousand years ago.

That compass used a magnet on a piece cork or straw floating on water. Look at the diagram of a compass. Why do you think the needle rests on a point? How do you think you could use a compass to find out which direction is east?

Compasses show direction because they line up with Earth's magnetism. What do you think might happen when another magnet is close to a compass? You can find out by switching on the coil you made in the Exploration and placing it at various points around a compass. **Try it!**

You've seen how a compass can be used to help you find a direction. What else do you think a compass could be used for?

Exploration:
Wrap a coil around a compass.

You need:

Cardboard
Scissors
Compass
Sandpaper
Enameled copper wire
Battery pack

❶ Cut out a cardboard rectangle a little larger than the compass. Then cut two notches in the rectangle. Tape the compass to the rectangle.

❷ Rub about 2 cm of each end of the copper wire with sandpaper.

❸ Attach one wire from the battery pack to one end of the copper wire.

❹ Wind the copper wire about 10 times around the compass, in one direction only.

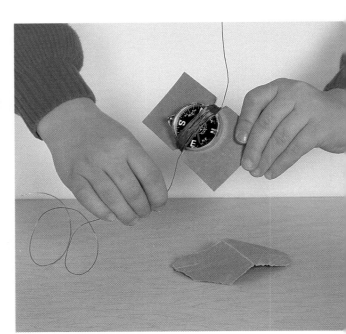

❺ Place the compass so that the needle is in line with the coil of wire. Touch the free end of the copper wire to the free wire from the battery pack. Record what happens. ✏️

Interpret your results.

• What did you observe when you completed the circuit?

• How was this effect similar to the effect you saw in the Exploration on page 30?

• You could use the coil wrapped around the compass as a test unit. What would you test for?

▲ A maglev train "floats" above the tracks.

▼ This electromagnet is separating iron and steel from other materials.

Closer to Home: Magnets at work

The magnets that hold notes onto your refrigerator door aren't the only magnets in your home. In fact, the refrigerator also has a magnet in its door latch.

The doorbell uses a magnet, a washing machine uses magnets, and stereos and VCRs use magnets. Any electric device with a motor or a loudspeaker uses magnets.

Magnets have many industrial uses, too. Recycling centers use <u>electromagnets</u>—magnets that are made using electric current—to pull the iron and steel from a pile of recycled trash. You made a small electromagnet in the first Exploration of this lesson. Electromagnets are also used in factories and junkyards to lift heavy loads.

Many countries are experimenting with trains that use magnetism to make the train hover just above the track. These trains, called maglev trains, are expected to be able to travel at speeds of over 500 kilometers (310 miles) per hour. Slower maglev trains are already operating in England and Germany.

- An electromagnet weighs much less than a regular magnet of the same strength. How could this be useful?

- How could magnetism lift a train above the railroad tracks?

Think!

What advantages are there in being able to turn a magnet on and off?

How Are Magnets Used to Make Electricity?

Nearly two hundred years ago, a scientist named Hans Oersted found out that electricity could cause magnetism. Other scientists thought that perhaps magnetism could cause electricity, too. About twenty years later, the scientist Michael Faraday found the answer. Magnetism can be used to make electricity. How?

Exploration:

Discover what happens when wires and magnets move.

❶ Find the meter in each diagram. It measures the amount of current in a wire. In which diagrams does the meter show that current is traveling through the wire?

❷ In what ways do the experiments in diagrams A and B differ? What conclusions can you draw?

❸ Look at diagrams C and D. Compare the readings on the meters. What differences are there in the experiments? How do they affect the reading on the meter? Record your answers. ✏

Interpret your results.

• When a wire moves between two magnets, what happens? How is the effect different when a magnet moves through a coil of wire?

• What makes the effect stronger?

• What other things do you think might make the effect stronger?

• What uses can you think of for the effect shown in the experiments?

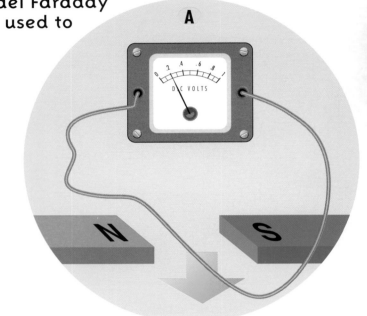

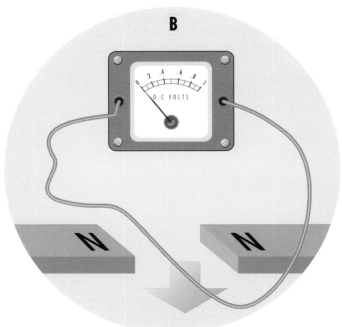

▲ The satellite on the left side of the picture is being pulled by the space shuttle *Atlantis.*

Exploration Connection:
Interpreting photographs

In September 1992 NASA conducted an interesting experiment using the space shuttle *Atlantis.* The picture shows the shuttle traveling at about 300 kilometers (185 miles) above Earth's surface. The shuttle is dragging a small satellite by a wire.

The crew of *Atlantis* reeled out the wire that connected the satellite and the shuttle. NASA planned to have the wire stretch 20 kilometers (12 1/2 miles).

Earth is a giant magnet. The shuttle was traveling past it—and so was the wire. What happens when a wire travels past a magnet? The crew hoped to make electricity. Although they couldn't extend the wire as far as they had planned, they did get the results they expected: They made electricity. Based on your Exploration, would the effect have been stronger if the wire had been longer? Explain your answer.

Closer to Home:
Free light for your bike

If you ride a bike at night, it should have lights at the front and the back. The front light lets you see where you're going. What's the back light for?

Most bicycle lights use batteries, like flashlights do. When the batteries run out, you have to get new ones. But there's another way to power the lights on a bike, using your own energy. You can use a <u>generator</u>—a device that turns motion into electricity.

A bike generator uses the bike's wheel to move a wire coil between the poles of a magnet. This makes an electric current, which powers the lights. The faster you ride, the more electricity the generator makes—and the brighter your lights will be.

- What are the advantages of using a generator on a bike? What are the disadvantages?

- How does using a generator help the environment?

Car batteries are rechargeable, but they don't have to be plugged into outlets like other rechargeable batteries. How do you think they get recharged?

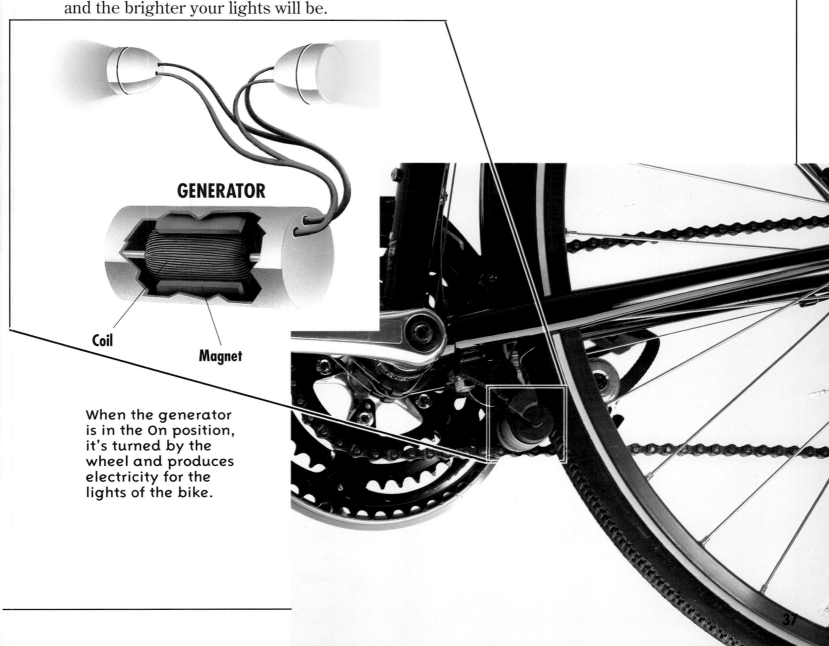

GENERATOR

Coil

Magnet

When the generator is in the On position, it's turned by the wheel and produces electricity for the lights of the bike.

How Do Power Plants Use Magnets to Generate Electricity?

Nearly all the electricity you use is produced by large generators that have coils of wire moving between magnets. The magnets are very strong. There's a lot of wire in the coils. The coils turn very fast. Where does the energy to turn the coils come from? How is it used to turn the coils?

Most generators use <u>turbines</u>. Turbines look a little like the sails of a windmill or the propeller of a ship. As water or gas moves past a turbine, the turbine turns. This motion is used to turn the coils of wire in a generator.

TURBINE

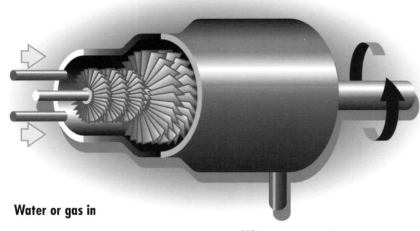

Water or gas in

Water or gas out

Most of the power plants in the United States use steam to push turbines. The most common way to make the steam is by burning a fuel such as coal, natural gas, or oil to boil water. These fuels are called fossil fuels, because they were formed over millions of years from plant fossils. There isn't enough fossil fuel on Earth to last forever. That's why people have looked for other ways to make steam.

Nuclear power plants use tiny amounts of a metal called uranium to start a nuclear reaction. The reaction releases heat, which is used to make steam.

▲ The blades of the windmills on this wind farm are turned by moving air. Each windmill contains a generator.

Nuclear power plants don't pollute the air, but their waste is very dangerous. A nuclear accident can be so dangerous that a large area around the accident may be poisoned for thousands of years.

Most fuels have to be mined and carried to a power plant. But some energy sources deliver themselves. Huge mirrors can be used to collect energy from the sun. This energy boils water to make the steam to run a generator. No fuels are used up, and there isn't any smoke or pollution from the power plant.

Other energy sources that deliver themselves are wind and water. Windmills have been used for over 1,400 years. Water power has been used for even longer. Many modern power plants use moving water instead of steam to turn turbines. Power plants that use water power are called <u>hydroelectric</u> plants.

► The mirrors at this solar power plant follow the sun. They focus the sun's rays on the water tower, where the heat is used to make steam.

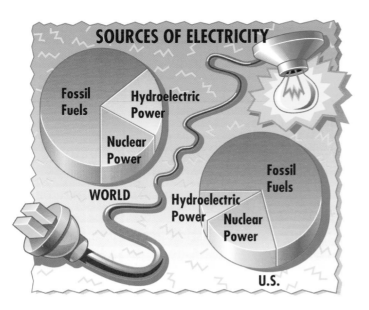

SOURCES OF ELECTRICITY

Fossil Fuels

Hydroelectric Power

Nuclear Power

WORLD

Hydroelectric Power

Fossil Fuels

Nuclear Power

U.S.

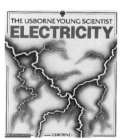

THE USBORNE YOUNG SCIENTIST
ELECTRICITY

Information Connection:
Using reference books

New ways of using the sun, the wind, and water to make electricity are being tried out all over the world. These sources of energy are free, and they're very clean because there are no waste products. But so far, these energy sources don't produce very much of the electricity that people use.

Look at the graphs showing the sources of electricity used in the United States and worldwide. Which source of power is used the most? Do you think this source will be the one most used in the future? Explain.

Power plants don't store electricity—they produce it when it's needed. At what time of day do you think most electricity is produced? You can find out by reading page 20 of *Electricity*.

▶ The coal in the freight cars will be burned at this power plant. The towers in the distance are cooling towers—they are used for cooling the hot water and steam from the plant.

◄ Hydroelectric power plants use moving water to turn turbines.

Closer to Home: Power and the planet

When you use an electric device, there doesn't seem to be any pollution or any change to the environment. But the energy that you use was generated in a power plant. Most likely, the power plant changes the environment in many ways.

Hydroelectric power sounds clean and safe—it uses water. But when a river or a lake is blocked off, the land is changed. These changes affect local wildlife. Power plants that use steam can put heated water into their surroundings. The heated water changes the environment. The plant and animal life that lived there before may not be able to live there anymore.

Whenever fossil fuels are burned—even in the cleanest power plants—there are wastes. The wastes contain chemicals that cause air pollution and acid rain. Burning any fossil fuel also produces carbon dioxide. Too much carbon dioxide may change the earth's climate. Drilling or mining for fossil fuels changes the environment, too, and transporting it by truck or train burns even more fossil fuel. If the fuel is moved by pipeline, the land has to be cleared for the pipes.

- In what ways do you think using power from the sun or wind might change the environment?

- How might getting electricity from a power plant to a town change the environment?

Think!

Why is energy conservation a good idea?

41

How Can Electricity Change to Motion?

A generator has a coil of wire turning between magnets. What do you think would happen if instead of turning the coil to make electricity, you sent electricity through the coil?

Exploration:
Make an electric motor.

You need:

Battery pack
Enameled wire
Sandpaper
Plastic rod
Tape
3 paper clips
Magnet

❶ Take a battery from the battery pack. Wrap the enameled wire around it 20 times to make a coil. Use sandpaper to make about 4 cm on each end of the wire shiny. Take the coil off the battery, and put the battery back in the pack.

❷ Push the plastic rod through the center of the coil. Tape the coil to keep it in place.

❸ Tape the ends of the coil to the rod, as shown in the second picture.

❹ Remove the wires with clips from the battery pack, but leave the connecting wire. Tape the two battery holders together.

❺ Bend two paper clips, as shown in the third picture. Clip them in the battery pack. Bend the other paper clip as shown. Clip it into the other end of the battery pack.

❻ Place the rod with the coil so that it rests in the bent paper clips. Move the two paper clips so that the bare wires from the coil each touch a separate paper clip.

❼ Hold a magnet at the side of the coil so it almost touches it. You may need to push the coil gently with a finger.

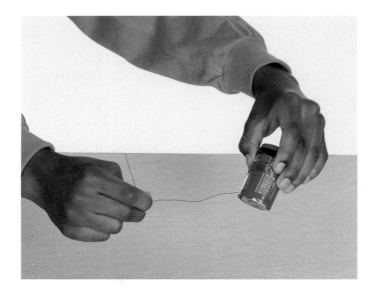

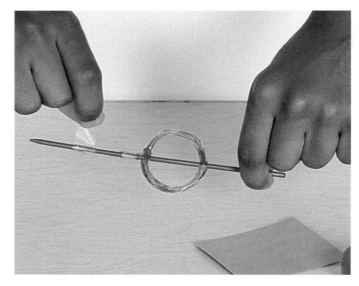

▼ When your device is finished, slowly move your magnet toward the coil. What happens?

Interpret your results.

- When the current traveled through the coil, it made magnetism. What effect did this magnetism have?

- What do you think would happen if you changed the pole of the magnet that is closest to the coil? **Try it!**

- What do you think would happen if you worked with another group to add more magnets? more battery packs? **Try it!**

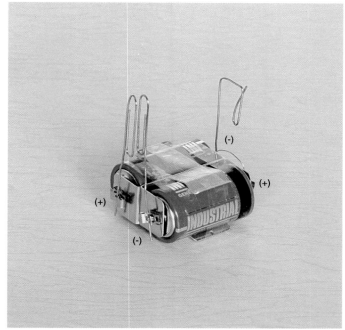

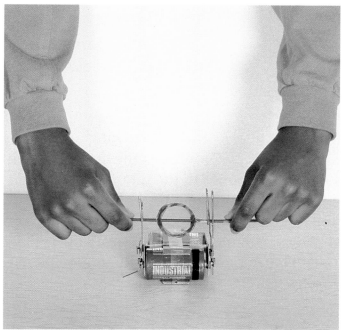

AN ELECTRIC MOTOR

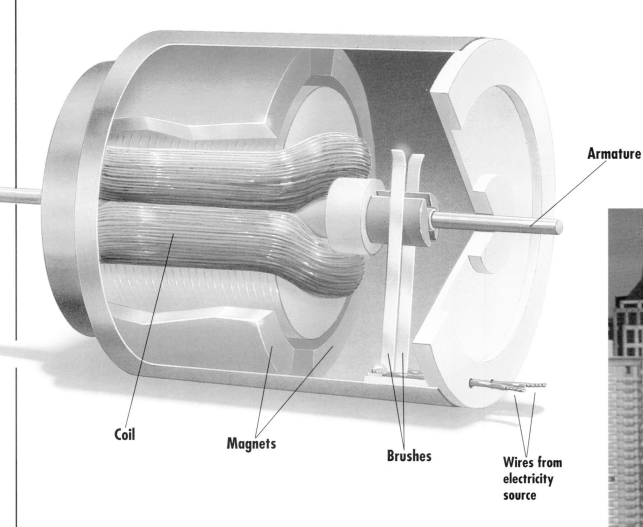

Armature

Coil

Magnets

Brushes

Wires from
electricity
source

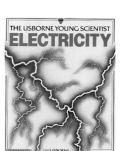

Exploration Connection:
Using reference books

You used electricity and magnetism to
make your motor turn. Look at the
diagram showing an electric motor.
How does the current reach the coil?
Look at the names of the motor parts. When you built
a motor, what did you use as an armature? What did
you use as brushes?

How else might you have used everyday objects to
build your motor? You can find out on page 15 of
Electricity.

◄ An electric motor turns the circular restaurant at the top of the Space Needle in Seattle, Washington, once every hour.

Closer to Home: Motorized

Your everyday life probably depends on electric motors. To get to school, you may take the subway, a bus, or a car. Subway trains run on electric motors. They get electricity from the tracks. Buses and cars have engines that run on gas, but they use electric motors to start the engines. The windshield wipers and heater fans use electric motors, too.

All kinds of devices around your home use electric motors similar to the one you built. Vacuum cleaners, tape players, electric clocks, washing machines—they all rely on electric motors. If you live in an apartment building with an elevator, you use an electric motor each time you go up or down.

- How are the motors in all these devices like the motor you made?

Think!

If you turn a motor by hand, do you generate electricity? Explain.

How Can Electricity Change to Sound?

You know how magnets and electricity can be used to make motion. One form of motion is sound. Sound is created by vibrations. Without motion, there would be no sound. How do you think you might use electricity to make sound?

Exploration:
Make a buzzer.

You need:

Battery pack
Electromagnet from Lesson 8
Paperclip
Clay

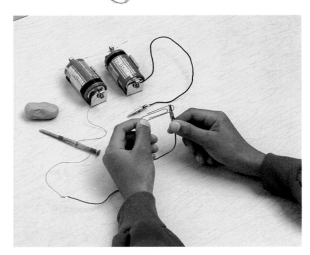

❶ Unclip the red wire from the battery pack. In its place, connect one end of the electromagnet wire to the battery pack.

❷ Twist together the free end of the electromagnet wire and the free end of the red wire. Clamp the paperclip into the alligator clip of the red wire.

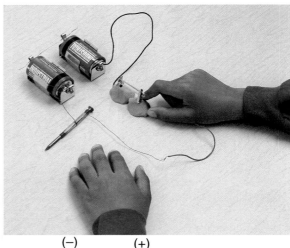

❸ Make a separate clay base for both alligator clips and the electromagnet.

❹ Position both alligator clips as shown in the photo. The paperclip should just touch the alligator clip that's on the black wire.

❺ Very slowly and carefully, move the electromagnet so that it almost touches the paper clip. Record what happens. ✐

Interpret your results.

• The electromagnet is part of a circuit. What path does the current take?

• When the electromagnet was turned on, what did it pull? What happened to the circuit?

• How did the circuit become complete again? What caused the sound you heard?

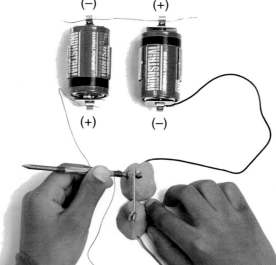

(−)   (+)

(+)   (−)

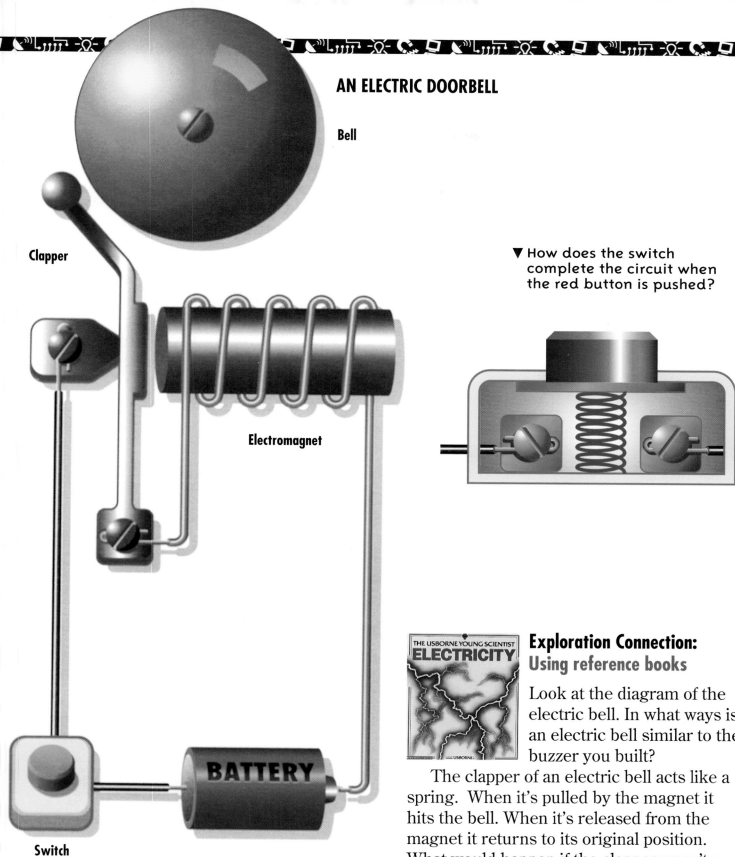

AN ELECTRIC DOORBELL

Bell

Clapper

Electromagnet

Switch

▲ This electric bell works the same way as the buzzer you made.

BATTERY

▼ How does the switch complete the circuit when the red button is pushed?

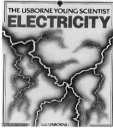

Exploration Connection:
Using reference books

Look at the diagram of the electric bell. In what ways is an electric bell similar to the buzzer you built?

The clapper of an electric bell acts like a spring. When it's pulled by the magnet it hits the bell. When it's released from the magnet it returns to its original position. What would happen if the clapper wasn't a spring?

Telephones use electromagnets to make sound. Look at the picture of the first telephone on page 26 of *Electricity*. Which part of the telephone is the electromagnet?

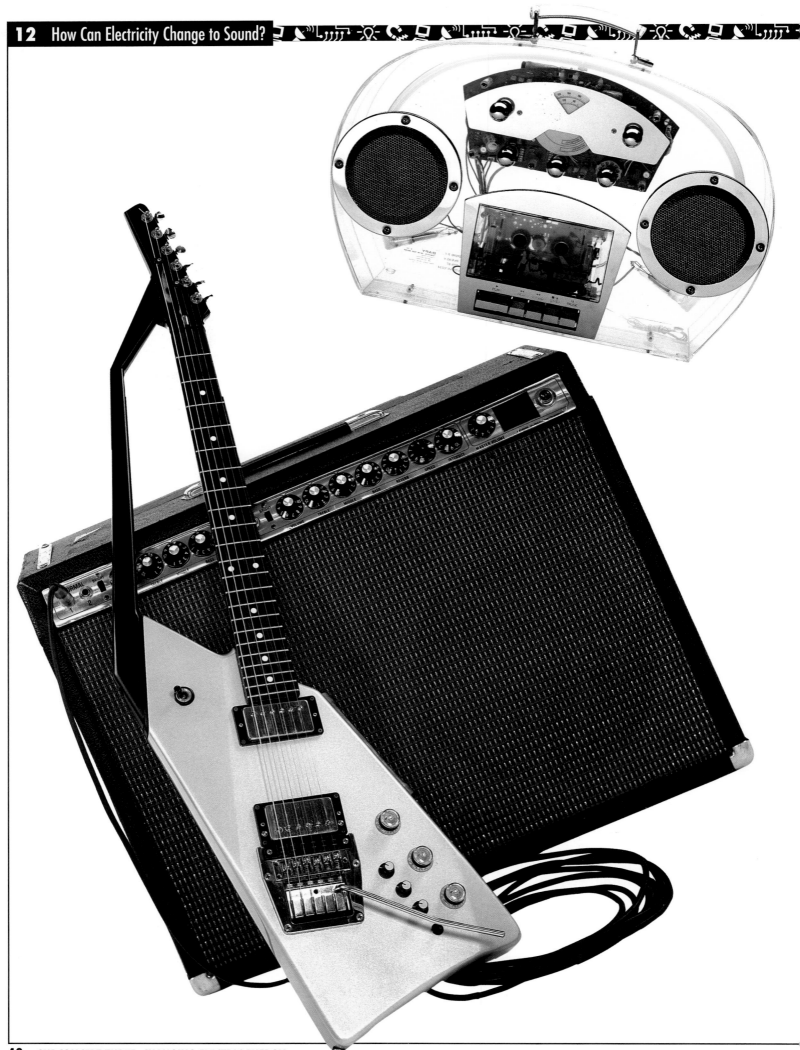

▼ Unless you're listening to live music, all the music you hear comes through speakers.

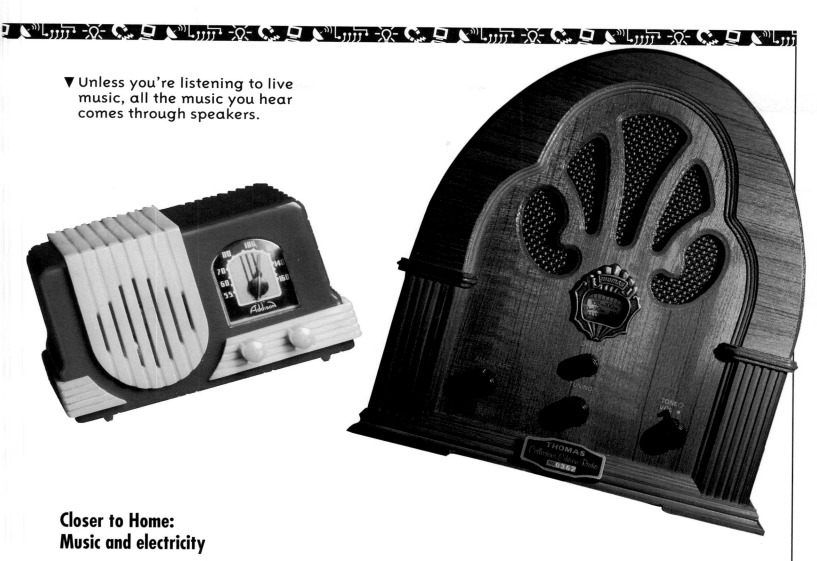

Closer to Home: Music and electricity

Who's your favorite singer? What's your favorite kind of music? You have thousands of choices—music plays a big part in people's lives. You can hear it on the radio, on television, and in films; you can play records, tapes, or CDs. But even though people have always loved music, they haven't always been able to listen to it whenever they wanted.

If you felt like listening to music a hundred years ago, you'd have had to go and hear people playing live. There weren't any radios or stereos then, and people didn't know how to record music. But as people began to learn more about electricity, that changed.

In 1920 the first radio show was broadcast. Five years later the first electric record players were sold. People were able to choose what music they wanted to hear—and when they wanted to hear it. By 1950 many people owned and used tape recorders.

The 1960s saw the invention of cassette tape recorders, and in the 1980s CDs became available. These days, records aren't as popular as tapes and CDs.

• In what ways did tape recorders change how people could listen to music?

In what way is a buzzer like a switch?

How Can Electricity Change to Heat?

When you built the buzzer, you needed the electric current to travel through the circuit easily. You used copper wires because copper is a good conductor. Not all conductors let the same amount of electricity travel through them. How do you think electricity affects a poor conductor?

Exploration:
Test electricity traveling through a graphite rod.

You need:
Flashlight bulb
Lamp holder
Battery pack
Graphite rod

❶ Screw the flashlight bulb into the lamp holder. Connect one clip from the battery pack to one of the holder's ends.

❷ Attach the other clip of the battery pack to one end of the graphite rod. Be careful not to snap the rod.

❸ Touch the free end of the lamp holder to the free end of the rod. Record the results. ✏

❹ Slowly slide the free terminal of the lamp holder along the graphite rod, toward the clip. What do you notice? ✏

Interpret your results.

• Compare the results of steps 3 and 4. How did the graphite rod change the results?

• The more electricity a lamp gets, the brighter it shines. How did the length of the graphite rod in the circuit change the amount of electricity the lamp got?

• Would copper give the same results in the experiment as the graphite did? **Try it!**

▲ The bars of an electric heater get hot when they carry electric current.

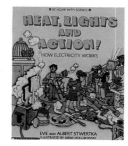

Exploration Connection:
Using reference books

What can you do when your hands are cold? You can hold them in front of an electric heater, or you can rub them together. Both of these methods will warm your hands up, and they both use the same thing to create heat—friction. There's friction any time two objects collide or rub against each other.

When electricity travels through a material that isn't a very good conductor, the electricity has to push its way through. It's a little like trying to walk through a crowded corridor—you get bumped and pushed. So when electricity goes through a material that isn't a very good conductor, there's friction. The friction makes heat.

Electricity can only travel through a complete circuit. So materials that are used in electric heaters must be able to carry electricity. They must be conductors—but not very good ones. How do you think these materials make heat? You can find out by reading pages 25–27 of *Heat, Lights and Action*!

Electric heaters of many kinds use special metals to make heat. Do you think these metals are very good conductors? What other material besides metals do you think might be used to make heat?

Exploration:
Observe current in a graphite rod.

You need:

Battery pack
Graphite rod
Candle

❶ Connect one alligator clip from the battery pack to one end of the graphite rod. Be careful not to snap the rod.

❷ Connect the other clip to a point on the graphite rod about 4 cm away from the first clip.

❸ Wait for about half a minute. Touch the graphite rod with the candle. Compare the temperature of the rod between the two clips with the temperature of the part of the rod that is left sticking out. Record your results.

Interpret your results.

• Do you think the results would have been the same if the battery pack had not been connected?

• What does an electric current do when it travels through graphite?

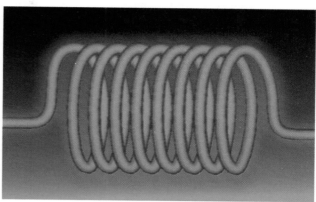

▼ Many electric devices, such as toasters and irons, use coils of wire to change electricity into heat.

Closer to Home: Everyday electric heat

There probably isn't a day that goes by without your using electricity to make heat. If you use an electric stove, a toaster, a hair dryer, or an iron in your home, you are running a current through materials that aren't very good conductors.

Many devices use coils of wire to make heat. A coil can make a long wire fit into a small space. All the heat produced by the long wire is made in the small space, so it can be used conveniently.

- It costs more to run an electric heater than a radio. Do you think it takes more electricity to produce heat or to produce sound?

- Oil, gas, and electricity are used to heat people's homes. What advantages are there in using electricity to heat a home?

Think!

Why would it be dangerous to use wires that aren't very good conductors to carry electricity to electric devices?

How Can Electricity Change to Light?

If you've ever looked inside an electric heater or a toaster, you may have seen that an electric heating device can also produce something else—light. Electric heaters use a lot of wire in the heating coils. If the wire was shorter, or if it carried more electricity, it would get hotter. What else do you think might happen?

Exploration:
Place a bulb in an electric circuit.

You need:
Flashlight bulb
Lamp holder
Battery pack

❶ Screw the bulb into the lamp holder.

❷ Connect the alligator clips from the battery pack to each terminal of the lamp holder as in the bottom photograph. Observe the bulb and feel it.

❸ Disconnect the wire attached between the two battery holders, and disconnect one of the wires that has an alligator clip. Attach that wire to the free terminal of the other battery holder as in the top photograph. Observe the bulb and feel it. ✎

Interpret your results.

- How was the brightness of the bulb affected by the number of batteries in the circuit?

- How does the amount of electricity affect the amount of light produced by a bulb?

- What did the bulb produce in addition to light?

- What happens when you increase the amount of electricity to a bulb?

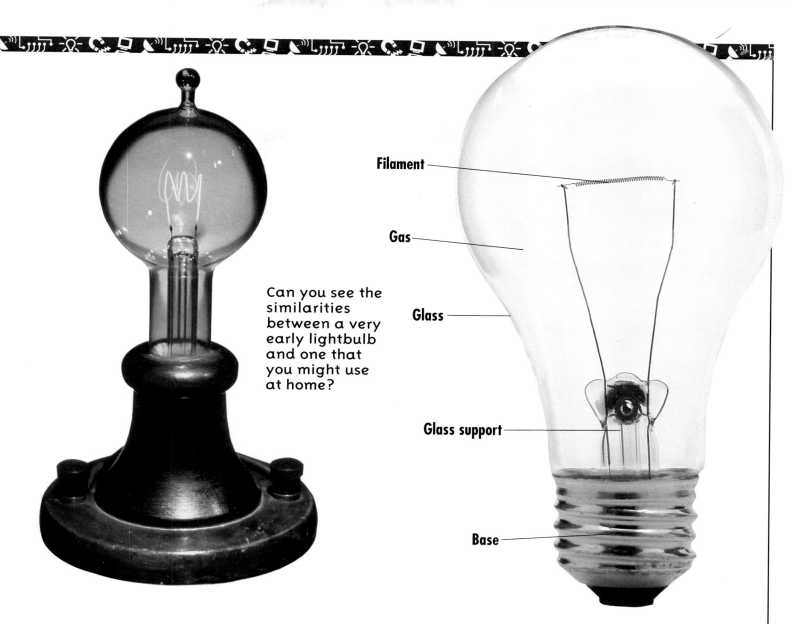

Can you see the similarities between a very early lightbulb and one that you might use at home?

Filament

Gas

Glass

Glass support

Base

Exploration Connection:
Interpreting diagrams

You've probably seen plenty of lightbulbs like the one shown in the diagram. Lightbulbs haven't changed very much since the first one was invented in 1879. The inventor, Thomas Edison, tried out more than 9,000 different materials to use as a filament. When a material gets hot enough, it glows red. If it gets even hotter, it glows white. Edison wanted to find a filament material that would get hot enough to give off white light. The materials that got that hot quickly burnt up in the air.

Edison knew that things can't burn without oxygen from the air. So he pumped the air out of a bulb. The filament didn't burn up, and it gave enough light to read by.

Within two years, Edison's filament was improved by Lewis Latimer. Do you think the wires Edison and Latimer used as filaments were good conductors?

Modern bulbs have a gas in them that prevents the filament from burning. The gas lets the heat pass from the filament to the glass of the bulb. This helps the filament last longer. The filament is made of a special metal that gives off lots of light when current passes through it. How do you think the electric current reaches the filament? When you coil wire, you can fit a lot of wire into a little space. Why do you think the wire of a filament is a coil?

The filament of a lightbulb is made of a material that uses electricity to make light. Think of the lightbulbs you use at home. They use a lot more electricity than flashlight bulbs do. Do the lightbulbs you use at home get hot? What happens if a bulb gets more electricity than it's designed for?

Exploration:
Vary the amount of electricity to a lamp.

You need:

Flashlight bulb
Lamp holder
3 battery packs

❶ Screw the flashlight bulb into the lamp holder.

❷ Remove the connecting wire between each of the battery packs. Leave on the wires that have the clips.

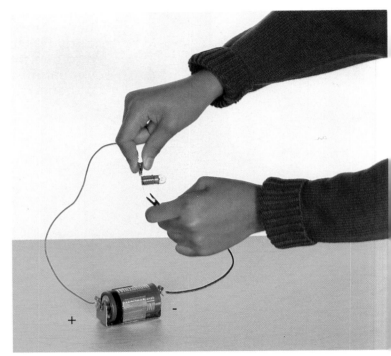

❸ Make a circuit that uses a single battery and the lamp. Observe the results. ✏

❹ Repeat step 3, adding on batteries one at a time to the circuit. Observe the results each time. ✏

Interpret your results.

• What happened as you added on more batteries to the circuit?

• The filament of a flashlight bulb is made of a metal that melts at very high temperatures. Look closely at the filament of the bulb you used. Do you think it got very hot?

• How is the lightbulb in this Exploration similar to a fuse?

▲ Electric light at night can be seen from space. Can you find the area where you live?

Closer to Home: Lighten up!

You can see a lot of different kinds of electric lights at school, at home, and in your neighborhood. Some of the lights—such as neon signs and traffic lights—aren't used to light up an area. They're used to give information. What other lights can you think of that give information?

The kind of bulb Edison invented is an <u>incandescent lamp</u>. All incandescent lamps have filaments, bases, and glass bulbs. What incandescent bulbs have you seen?

Some electric lamps don't have filaments. Instead, electricity passes through a gas in the bulb. Neon lamps work this way. The electric current causes the neon gas to shine. The most common kind of lamp without a filament is the <u>fluorescent lamp</u>. It uses less electricity than an incandescent lamp, and it doesn't get hot.

The LEDs you used in some of the Explorations aren't incandescent. They aren't fluorescent, either. The light they give comes from crystals that glow when electricity passes through them. They don't get hot and they use very little electricity— but they don't make very much light, either.

- Why do schools, hospitals, and government offices use fluorescent lamps instead of incandescent lamps?

- What are some uses for LEDs?

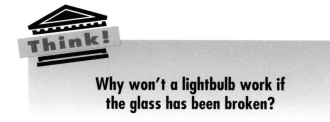

Think!

Why won't a lightbulb work if the glass has been broken?

Identify Problems: Designing an Electric Toy

Think Tank Road Map

In the days before electricity, toys didn't speak or light up. These days toy makers can use electricity from several sources—generators, batteries, or solar cells—to power their toys.

A toy designer must decide what he or she wants the toy to do, then solve all the problems involved in building it.

 In Lesson 15 you'll identify the problems you'd have designing a toy that moves, lights up, or makes sounds.

 In Lesson 16 you'll identify some possible solutions to these problems.

 In Lesson 17 you'll design an electric toy. Then you'll make a model based on your design.

You may also want to review the video.

Problem: An exciting new movie is opening this summer. The movie company has asked you and your team to design a special toy to advertise the movie. The toy must use electricity to move, light up, or make sounds. Your team must put together a plan that describes the toy and how it will work.

 These questions will help you make a list of the problems you might have while trying to design your toy:

1
What have you already learned about electricity that could help you solve some of the problems you'll face?

2
What are some sources of electricity that could power a toy? Which source will you use?

3
What materials will you need to build a toy? Will they be safe to play with?

4
Will the toy light up, make noise or move around? Will it do all three?

5
How will your toy advertise the movie?

6
These pages show some fun inventions that run on electricity. They're small enough to carry around with you. As you study the pictures, ask yourself: How do these devices use electricity?

◀ **Tape Player** This small tape player uses batteries as a power supply. A motor moves the tape and an amplifier makes the sound as soft or loud as you like. When these stereos first came out, people were amazed that such small machines could produce so much sound.

▶ **Bicycle Light** When it starts to get dark, a bicycle light is a great thing to have. The back tire runs a small generator that makes enough electricity to power the light. The faster you go, the brighter the light gets.

◀ **Hat Fan** The inventor of this device solved two problems at once. The hat protects your head and face from the sun and makes a cool breeze on hot summer days. The fan can be powered by batteries or a solar cell.

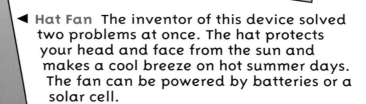

Think!

How can knowing how these devices use electricity help you design your toy?

Find Solutions: Designing an Electric Toy

You've just identified some problems you'll face in designing an electric toy. Now you'll identify possible solutions to those problems by studying another electrical device—the hat fan. Studying how an inventor made a fun, safe toy might help you and your team find solutions to designing your own.

What are solar cells?

Some electric toys aren't powered by batteries or generators. They carry solar cells and are powered by energy from the sun. Solar cells are made of silicon, one of the materials in common beach sand.

Solar cells change sunlight into electricity, and in many ways, they're an ideal source of power. Unlike batteries, solar cells don't contain harmful chemicals and don't wear out. Unlike generators, they don't need a source of motion (like a bicycle tire) to power them. They don't pollute, they don't use up the Earth's natural resources, and they're silent. All they need is sunlight.

Large solar cells are expensive, so solar electricity is still not very popular for big energy needs. For small inventions like the hat fan, however, solar cells can be a great source of energy.

1

Record the problems you listed in the last lesson. Beside each of them, try to list a similar problem solved by the designers of the hat fan.

2

Study the diagram of the hat fan. Why was it important to place the fan in the position it's in? How does the design of the hat let the air blow in?

3

How does the fan work? What powers the motor? How is the battery connected to the fan? Why do the fan's wires run on the inside of the hat?

4

Record the solutions the designers of the hat fan came up with. Record some possible solutions to your own toy designing problems.

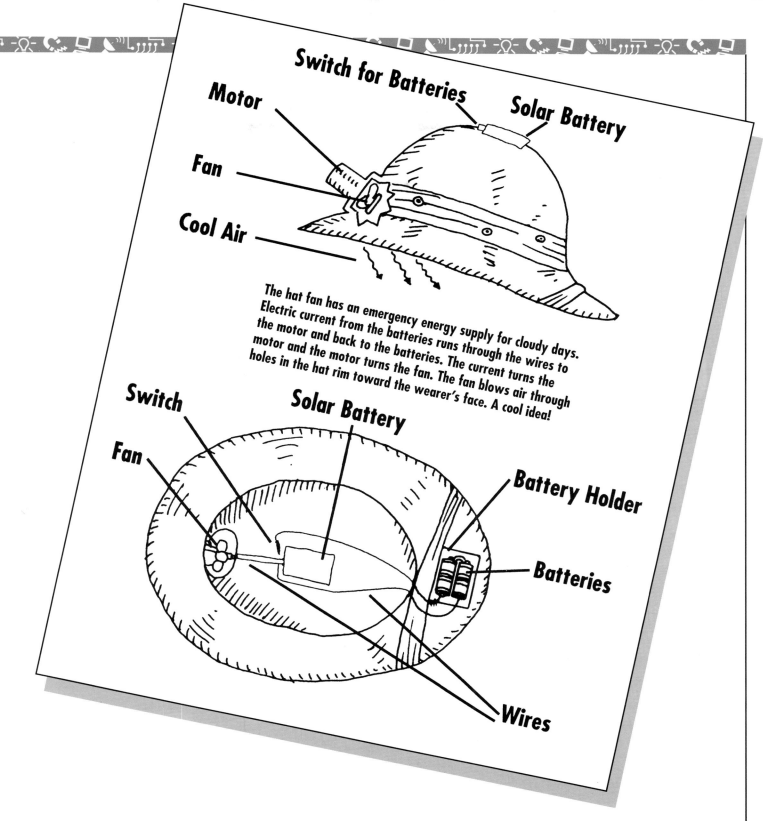

Switch for Batteries

Motor

Solar Battery

Fan

Cool Air

The hat fan has an emergency energy supply for cloudy days. Electric current from the batteries runs through the wires to the motor and back to the batteries. The current turns the motor and the motor turns the fan. The fan blows air through holes in the hat rim toward the wearer's face. A cool idea!

Switch

Solar Battery

Fan

Battery Holder

Batteries

Wires

How can looking at the design of the hat fan help you design your electric toy?

Other resources you can check:

• To find out more about electricity: *Science with Batteries* by Paul Shipton. Usborne Publishing, 1993.

• To find out how things work: *Energy & Power* by Richard Spurgeon and Mike Flood. Usborne Publishing, 1990.

THINK TANK

Make Models: Designing an Electric Toy

You and your team have identified problems you'll face in designing an electric toy to advertise a new movie. You've also identified possible solutions to some of those problems. Now it's time to make a model of your toy.

Possible models for your electric toy:

Diagram Use the diagrams in the previous lessons to help you draw a large, detailed diagram of your toy. Be sure to label the diagram to explain how your toy works.

3-Dimensional Model Use cardboard, batteries, wires or other materials to create a model of your toy.

Written Description Write an advertisement for your toy. Describe every detail: its parts, size, and materials. Make sure you clearly explain how it moves, lights up, or makes sound.

Computer Graphics Use a graphics program to design the toy on a computer.

Oral Presentation Give a speech about your toy as though you were describing it to the movie company.

1

Work with your team to design your electric toy. List all the parts your toy will have and the things it will be able to do. Make sure your design includes these things.

2

Go back to lessons 11, 12, and 14 to review how electricity can be used to make motion, sound, or light. Study the diagrams in those lessons.

3

Will your power source be batteries, a generator or a solar cell? Will you need to use parallel or series circuits to connect the parts that run on electricity?

4

How will you switch your toy on and off? If your toy moves *and* lights up, will the different parts have different switches?

5

Make a model of your design. Gather your materials and go to work.

6

Look at all the models your class made. Did everybody have the same problems and solutions?

7

What were the most important things you learned in this unit that helped you design an electric toy?

Resources for designing your electric toy:

• Your journals and LabMats from this unit are filled with helpful information about electricity.

• Look back at the information in lessons 1–14 of this *Student's Map to Exploration.*

• The reference books you've used in this unit can help.

• How did the Science Sleuths investigate electrical energy?

• If you run into trouble with your design, ask another team for input.

Think!

How did making a model of your toy help you discover new problems and solutions?

FOR SCIENCE BROWSERS

How Much Electricity Does It Take to Run a Computer?

excerpt from *Ranger Rick*

A computer uses about as much electricity as a bright light bulb. This may not seem like a lot. But there are about 35 million personal computers in the United States. And all together, they use a lot of "juice."

Luckily the U.S. government has started a project called "Energy Star Computers." This project helps computer companies find ways to reduce the amount of energy needed to run computers. If your family is buying a new computer, look for one with an "Energy Star" label. The computer will work just as well as others, but it'll use less electricity.

One neat way that an Energy Star computer saves electricity is by "going to sleep." When the computer is on but no one is using it, it automatically uses less electricity—sometimes as little as 30 watts instead of 100 watts. Then when you touch the keyboard, the computer "wakes up" and works as usual.
—*January 1994*

© Danielle Jones 1994

Lightning: Nature's High-Voltage Spectacle

by William R. Newcott

excerpt from *National Geographic*

© Thomas Ives

It is a river of electricity rushing through a canyon of air. Careering as fast as 100,000 miles a second, lightning sears wild and unstoppable through twisted channels as long as ten miles.

Drag your shoes along a carpet. You become a thundercloud. Your scuffing pulls electrons from the fabric, giving you a negative charge. Reach for a metal doorknob. It, like the earth under a thundercloud, is positively charged. Since opposites attract, when you get close enough, zap—the excess electrons stream to the knob in a miniature bolt.

Looking for a Charge

Summoned by scientists who launched a three-foot-high rocket toward the belly of a passing thundercloud, a bolt of lightning crashes into Mosquito Lagoon near Florida's Kennedy Space Center.

From the rocket's tail a spool of copper wire unwound, triggering the strike and creating an artificial path for the cloud's electric charge.

Rocket launches provide the best chance for scientists to measure lightning's electric current under somewhat controlled conditions. However, risks still loom: To eliminate the danger of the current following wires from the launch pad onto the control trailer, scientists ignite rocket engines by blowing into a tube linked to a pneumatic switch on the pad.

Photography is another tool in the study of lightning, illustrating the numerous return strokes that to the human eye appear as a single flash. A still camera panned from left to right with the shutter open reveals the first stroke of a flash (above), with its characteristic branches, and some 20 subsequent strokes through the same air channel. Such repeat surges make lightning seem to flicker.
—*July 1993* ☀️

Swimming in the Current

Electric eels aren't the only animals that can generate an electric charge. About 500 species of fish do, including certain catfish and stingray species.

© Peter Menzel

Is Power a Problem?

by Chana Freiman
excerpt from *SuperScience Blue*

The Shocking Truth
Benjamin Franklin's kite wasn't zapped by a bolt of lightning. He flew the kite before the thunderstorm, collecting electric charges from the air. The charges traveled down a wet string to the famous key. A lightning bolt would have seriously damaged the kite, the string, the key, and Ben.

A two-story house stands alone on a wooded hillside. No one lives in it. Who could? It has no furniture —not even plaster to cover the walls!

This strange house is part of an experiment that began in 1988. Scientists built it to measure a not-so-strange force—one that's in all homes everywhere, including yours.

"Magnetic fields (MFs) are very common," says Gary Johnson, an engineer.

All electric things give off MFs when used—toasters, TVs, hair dryers. They also may give off electric fields (EFs).

"You can't see these fields," Gary told us. "But they are there whenever you use electricity."

Harmful Or Harmless?

Why wire up a special house to measure fields? About 15 years ago, scientist Nancy Wertheimer (WERT-hi-mer) began visiting kids in Denver, Colorado, who had cancer. She noticed that kids who lived near power lines were twice as likely to have cancer as kids who didn't. (Power lines carry electricity from power generators to your home, school, and other places.)

Nancy's data raised an important question: Can MFs and EFs cause health problems? Or are they harmless?

So far, no one has proof either way. But data from the test house will show where and how strong MFs are in a typical home. Other tests may prove whether or not these levels are harmful. And if

so, engineers like Gary can decide how to make the fields safer.

That's a big "if." Remember: Power lines may have nothing to do with cancer.

"One explanation could be that lots of power lines mean lots of people live in the area," Gary told us, "which means more traffic and more car exhaust fumes."

The fumes or other variables (factors) could be the link to cancer —not the power lines.

Plus, fields are strongest near their source. Then they drop off— fast. And humans rarely stand right next to strong fields for long periods of time.

For that reason, scientists wired the test house with regular appliances —including a refrigerator, oven, air conditioner, TV, and computer. You come in close contact with gadgets like these every day.

So far, biologists (life scientists) have found that magnetic fields can

cause changes in cells. But the changes may not be harmful.

"What we do know is that there's enough concern to study the problem further," Nancy says. "But there's *not* enough to be alarmed." —*March 1992* 🔆

© J.P. Nacivet/Leo de Wys Inc.

Empowering Algae—To Make Electricity, That Is

by Otis Port
excerpt from *Business Week*

Peter Spacek

Maybe next we'll grow our own electricity. Paul Jenkins, an engineering professor at the University of the West in Bristol, England, already does. He harvests kilowatts of power from lowly algae.

His gadget, called Biocoil, produces bumper crops of algae by suspending the organisms in a nutrient broth and circulating it through a clear plastic tube warmed by sunlight. Some algae are continuously siphoned off, filtered, dried, then chopped into fine particles. These are pressurized and injected into a diesel engine, providing 85% of its fuel as it drives an electrical generator. The carbon dioxide produced by the engine is recycled back to the Biocoil to feed the algae. Jenkins says the system should generate power as cheap as that from new coal-fired plants. —*February 1993* 🔆

Electric Messages Electricity has changed the way people live. The changes began in the 1840s, when the telegraph changed the way people communicate. Messages sent by Morse code over an electric wire could travel 100 million times faster than Pony Express riders, who carried mail on horseback.

Fast as a Bullet

by Mark Henricks
excerpt from *Boys' Life*

Every afternoon, Herb Alban drives a bullet. He's the engineer on the fastest train in America.

Alban controls the 6,000-horsepower locomotive that pulls the Metroliner Express out of Washington, D.C. His train hits 75 miles per hour, then 80...90...100...110. Before it pulls in to New York City, Alban's

Fuji, rocket along at 165 m.p.h.

Europe has bullet trains too. The world's fastest is the French "TGV." That stands for *train a grande vitesse,* which is French for "high-speed train." Every day, TGV's convey passengers to their destinations at speeds of 186 m.p.h. The fastest trip ever was in May 1990, when a TGV reached *320 m.p.h.* on a test run.

passenger-filled train will top 125 m.p.h.

"I like speed," Alban says.

Trains like Alban's are called supertrains. All over the world, they shoot between cities at amazing speeds.

Rockets on Rails

Supertrains first ran 25 years ago in Japan. They were called "bullet trains" because of their sleek design. Today, trains in Japan, like the one shown above zooming past Mount

"It's astonishing," says Joseph Vranich, a Virginia train expert who recently rode a new supertrain in Spain. He says the 150-m.p.h. journey over mountains was "as smooth as glass."

Super Safety Records

Supertrains are safe. The sharp-nosed bullet trains in Japan have carried a total of three billion passengers, and there has never been a fatal accident. Supertrains in Europe also have great safety records.

Many travelers would rather travel by supertrain than by airplane. Every seat on a supertrain is wide and comfortable. The trains have big windows from which to look out. In some trains, attendants serve food and drinks.

Putting Trains on a Diet

Most older trains burn diesel fuel. But supertrains are powered by electricity, like a light bulb. They get the power from wires that run above the trains.

When a supertrain shoots by, you won't hear any clickety-clack. The sections of a supertrain track are welded into one smooth piece. That keeps the train stable at high speeds.

Supertrain locomotives and cars are designed to slice through the wind. To squeeze out even more speed, designers put supertrains on a diet. The newest French TGV's are made of plastic, graphite and titanium. They are tons lighter than older trains—and faster.

Magnet Power

The newest train technology is called "maglev," which is short for magnetic levitation. To see how maglev works, put two magnets together. The positive pole attracts the negative pole. But if you try to push the positive poles together, they pull back.

With maglev technology, magnets in the train push against magnets in the track to hold up the train. By switching magnets on and off rapidly, the floating train can move without touching the ground.

And does it move! Maglev trains could one day be the high-speed champs. The experimental German Transrapid maglev train can travel at more than 300 m.p.h.

The first maglev train in America is to open in late 1998 to early 1999 in Orlando, Fla. A 13.5 mile ride will take just seven minutes at a top speed of 250 m.p.h.

Are Supertrains Earth-Friendly?

The last thing the environment needs is another smoke-belching, noisy train. Supertrains are anything but that.

To reach their incredible speeds, supertrains use electricity. They draw power through overhead lines, called catenaries, from the same electric utility plants that supply your house with electricity.

Generating electric power does cause pollution. But controlling pollution at a power plant is easier than on a rolling, diesel-powered locomotive.

The biggest damage to the earth from supertrains may come from the track itself. For speed, supertrain tracks must be much straighter than regular railroads. They must go through, rather than around, forests, for example.

Some existing tracks could be upgraded to supertrain quality. And other supertracks could be built down the middle of divided highways.

Because they ride on smooth rails, supertrains are quieter than regular trains. Maglev trains, which don't touch the ground at all, make no more noise than a car.
—*November 1993* ☀

An Old Idea
The electric car isn't a new invention. The first electric cars were invented in Europe in the 1800s. By the late 1800s, Americans were driving more electric cars than gasoline-powered cars.

GLOSSARY

Concept vocabulary and other technical terms

charge [chärj]: *n.* A quality of electricity that can be either positive or negative; similar charges repel each other and opposite charges attract each other.

circuit [sur' • kit]: *n.* The path through which an electric current travels; current will not travel unless a circuit is complete and has no breaks.

conductor [kən • duk' • tər]: *n.* An object or material that will allow an electric current to travel through it.

current [kur' • ənt]: *n.* Electricity that moves through a circuit.

electromagnet [i • lek • trō • mag' • nət]: *n.* A magnet that relies on electric current to create magnetism; most electromagnets are made of wire coiled around a piece of iron.

filament [fil' • ə • mənt]: *n.* The thin conductor in an incandescent lamp that glows brightly when electric current travels through it.

fluorescent lamp [flôr • es' • ənt lamp]: *n.* A lamp without a filament, in which electricity passes through a gas and produces an invisible light; a special coating on the inside of the glass changes the light to visible light.

fossil fuel [fos' • əl fyoo' • əl]: *n.* Any fuel formed from the remains of prehistoric life; oil, natural gas, and coal are fossil fuels.

fuse [fyooz]: *n.* A thin wire placed in a circuit to prevent too much electricity from traveling through the circuit; the fuse melts and breaks the circuit if it has to carry too much electricity.

generator [jen' • ə • rā • tər]: *n.* A machine that converts one form of energy into another, especially mechanical energy into electrical energy.

hydroelectric power [hī • drō • i • lek' • trik pou' • ər]: *n.* Electricity produced by water turning the turbine of a generator.

incandescent lamp [in • kən • des' • ənt lamp]: *n.* A lamp that uses electricity to make a filament glow brightly.

magnetic pole [mag • net' • ik pōl]: *n.*
1. Either of the two parts of a magnet where the magnetic force is the greatest; the poles of a bar magnet or a horseshoe magnet are at each end.
2. The points on the earth where the magnetic force is greatest; they are fairly close to the North Pole and the South Pole.

parallel circuit [par' • ə • lel sûr' • kit]: *n.* A circuit in which the current travels along two or more separate paths to different devices; the current travels through each part of the circuit at the same time.

series circuit [sēr' • ēz sûr' • kit]: *n.* A circuit in which the current travels along a single path to two or more electric devices; the current travels through each part of the circuit in turn.

static electricity [stat' • ik i • lek • tris' • ə • tē]: *n.* A single electric charge that doesn't move.

turbine [tûr' • bīn]: *n.* The part of a generator that uses the motion of water, steam, or wind to turn the coils or magnets in the generator.

a	add, map	ī	ice, write	û(r)	burn, term
ā	ace, rate	o	odd, hot	yoo	fuse, few
â(r)	care, air	ō	open, so	ə	a in above
ä	palm, father	ô	order, jaw		e in sicken
e	end, pet	oͦo	took, full		i in possible
ē	equal, tree	oo	pool, food		o in melon
i	it, give	u	up, done		u in circus

Page references in *italics* indicate illustrations, photographs, and tables.